Patchwork Crochet™

Table of Contents

AF190539

Sweet Dreams
Baby Blanket, *page 35*

Introduction

Patchwork Single Crochet

Patchwork has been described as the method of creating a fabric piece by piece, just as we create a house brick by brick or board by board. The early settlers created patchwork quilts by using every scrap of fabric leftover from their sewing projects. Granny squares were originally created to use leftover bits of yarn, then the individual squares were either sewn or crocheted together into warm, cozy blankets.

Several years ago, I became intrigued with Patchwork Knitting, then later on Tunisian Patchwork. I loved the idea of being able to create interesting items with little blocks and use color in different ways, and I really loved the join-as-you-go aspect of this particular type of Patchwork.

I did workshops on both Knitting Patchwork and Tunisian Patchwork, and while most students loved trying new ideas, some crocheters found the Tunisian method difficult. I started experimenting with creating the same look using simple single crochet, and this book is the result. I am really excited about it, and I hope that the ideas in this book will jump-start your creativity and you will come up with new and exciting ideas of your own.

Things You Need to Know About Patchwork Crochet

There are basically two shapes used in this book: the square and the shell.

All of the projects are created using one of these shapes. The squares can be used in two different ways. The Basic Square will just be built from side to side and column to column to create your fabric. If the Basic Square is turned to resemble a diamond shape, the building blocks are created a little differently and will require some fill-in shapes. I will refer to this shape as On Point Square.

I've included instructions and given specific yarns, crochet hooks and stitches used for each piece. Unless changes or substitutions are made, projects should appear just as those pictured. After you learn the technique, I encourage you, however, to let your imagination take over. Change colorways, mix and match techniques, or try some different ways of building your fabric. Have fun and create something that is truly your own.

Helpful Hints

1. Before you begin your project, it is very helpful to make one small square or shell to check your gauge and to help in placement.

2. There are a lot of ends created using this method. It is very helpful, after a few pieces are made, to take the time to weave in a few ends rather than leaving them loose until the end. It is also possible to work over the yarn tail when joining at the beginning of a row.

3. When working the shell motifs for a blanket or garment, it is necessary to use side fillers. When working a hat or a bag in the shell motif, it is not necessary to make side fillers, but top and bottom fillers are necessary.

Patchwork Squares

Pattern Notes

Chain-1 at end of row does not count as a stitch.

Stitch counts shown in Basic Square are same for all Squares.

When foundation row of any Square is created with chains and stitches, "chs" of row 1 will be single crochet or chains. Work in back loops of stitches of foundation row where appropriate.

Basic Square

Foundation row: Ch 34.

Row 1 (WS): Working in **back bar of chs** *(see illustration)*, sc in 2nd ch from hook, sc in each of first 15 chs, **sc dec** *(see Stitch Guide)* in next 3 chs, sc in each of last 15 chs, ch 1, turn. *(31 sc)*

Back Bar of Chain

Row 2: Sc in each of first 14 sc, sc dec in next 3 sc, sc in each of last 14 sc, ch 1, turn. *(29 sc)*

Row 3: Sc in each of first 13 sc, sc dec in next 3 sc, sc in each of last 13 sc, ch 1, turn. *(27 sc)*

Row 4: Sc in each of first 12 sc, sc dec in next 3 sc, sc in each of last 12 sc, ch 1, turn. *(25 sc)*

Row 5: Sc in each of first 11 sc, sc dec in next 3 sc, sc in each of last 11 sc, ch 1, turn. *(23 sc)*

Row 6: Sc in each of first 10 sc, sc dec in next 3 sc, sc in each of last 10 sc, ch 1, turn. *(21 sc)*

Row 7: Sc in each of first 9 sc, sc dec in next 3 sc, sc in each of last 9 sc, ch 1, turn. *(19 sc)*

Row 8: Sc in each of first 8 sc, sc dec in next 3 sc, sc in each of last 8 sc, ch 1, turn. *(17 sc)*

Row 9: Sc in each of first 7 sc, sc dec in next 3 sc, sc in each of last 7 sc, ch 1, turn. *(15 sc)*

Row 10: Sc in each of first 6 sc, sc dec in next 3 sc, sc in each of last 6 sc, ch 1, turn. *(13 sc)*

Row 11: Sc in each of first 5 sc, sc dec in next 3 sc, sc in each of last 5 sc, ch 1, turn. *(11 sc)*

Row 12: Sc in each of first 4 sc, sc dec in next 3 sc, sc in each of last 4 sc, ch 1, turn. *(9 sc)*

Row 13: Sc in each of first 3 sc, sc dec in next 3 sc, sc in each of last 3 sc, ch 1, turn. *(7 sc)*

Row 14: Sc in each of first 2 sc, sc dec in next 3 sc, sc in each of last 2 sc, ch 1, turn. *(5 sc)*

Row 15: Sc in next sc, sc dec in next 3 sc, sc in last sc, ch 1, turn. *(3 sc)*

Row 16: Sc dec in 3 sc. *(1 sc)*

2-Color Square

When changing colors, do not fasten off after each color change; carry yarn not in use up sides, twisting new color with last color worked.

Foundation row: With first color, ch 34.

Row 1 (WS): Working in **back bar of chs** *(see illustration)*, sc in 2nd ch from hook, sc in each of first 15 chs, sc dec in next 3 chs, sc in each of last 15 chs, **change color** *(see Stitch Guide)* in last ch to 2nd color, ch 1, turn.

Row 2: Sc in each of first 14 sc, sc dec in next 3 sc, sc in each of last 14 sc, ch 1, turn.

Row 3: Sc in each of last 13 sc, sc dec in next 3 sc, sc in each of last 13 sc, change color to first color, ch 1, turn.

Row 4: Sc in each of first 12 sc, sc dec in next 3 sc, sc in each of last 12 sc, ch 1, turn.

Row 5: Sc in each of first 11 sc, sc dec in next 3 sc, sc in each of last 11 sc, change color to 2nd color, ch 1, turn.

Row 6: Sc in each of first 10 sc, sc dec in next 3 sc, sc in each of last 10 sc, ch 1, turn.

Row 7: Sc in each of first 9 sc, sc dec in next 3 sc, sc in each of last 9 sc, change color to first color, ch 1, turn.

Row 8: Sc in each of first 8 sc, sc dec in next 3 sc, sc in each of last 8 sc, ch 1, turn.

Row 9: Sc in each of first 7 sc, sc dec in next 3 sc, sc in each of last 7 sc, change color to 2nd color, ch 1, turn.

Row 10: Sc in each of first 6 sc, sc dec in next 3 sc, sc in each of last 6 sc, ch 1, turn.

Row 11: Sc in each of first 5 sc, sc dec in next 3 sc, sc in each of last 5 sc, change color to first color, ch 1, turn.

Row 12: Sc in each of first 4 sc, sc dec in next 3 sc, sc in each of last 4 sc, ch 1, turn.

Row 13: Sc in each of first 3 sc, sc dec in next 3 sc, sc in each of last 3 sc, change color to 2nd color, ch 1, turn.

Row 14: Sc in each of first 2 sc, sc dec in next 3 sc, sc in each of last 2 sc, ch 1, turn.

Row 15: Sc in next sc, sc dec in next 3 sc, sc in last sc, change color to first color, fasten off 2nd color, turn.

Row 16: Sc dec in 3 sc.

Textured Square

Work same as Basic Square, working rows 2–16 in **back lps** *(see Stitch Guide)*. ●

Basic Square

Textured Square

2-Color Square

Photography by Chris Hubert

Captivating Cardi

Skill Level

 INTERMEDIATE

Finished Sizes

Instructions given fit woman's size small; changes for medium, large, X-large and 2X-large are in [ ].

Finished Measurement

Bust: 33½ [40, 46½, 53, 59½] inches

Materials

- Lion Brand Coboo light (DK) weight cotton/rayon yarn (3½ oz/232 yds/100g per ball): **3 LIGHT**
    6 [8, 10, 12, 14] balls #835-109 steel blue
    2 [2, 3, 3, 4] balls #835-123 tan
- Size H/8/5mm crochet hook or size needed to obtain gauge
- Size G/6/4mm hook for cuffs only
- Stitch markers
- Tapestry needle
- ¾-inch button: 1
- Rustproof pins

Gauge

Shell: 6½ inches wide

Dc: 18 sts = 4 inches

Pattern Notes

Before stitching begins, see Pattern Notes on page 3.

Cardi is made of Shells and Half Shells worked with a join-as-you-go technique.

Weave in loose ends as work progresses.

Colors change at end of every odd-numbered row. Do not fasten off after each color change; carry yarn not in use up sides, twisting new color with last color worked.

Place markers where indicated and remove them as work progresses unless otherwise stated.

Use larger hook for all parts except cuff, which uses the G hook.

Chain-2 at beginning of row counts as first double crochet.

Chain-3 at beginning of row counts as first double crochet.

Special Stitch

Single crochet join (sc join): Place a slip knot on hook, insert hook in indicated st, yo, pull up a lp, yo and draw through both lps on hook.

Cardi

Row 1

Shell

Make 5 [6, 7, 8, 9].

Foundation row: With steel blue and **larger hook** *(see Pattern Notes)*, ch 32.

Row 1 (WS): Working in **back bars of chs** *(see illustration on page 3)*, sc in 2nd ch from hook and in each ch across, **change color** *(see Stitch Guide and Pattern Notes)* to tan, turn. *(31 sc)*

Row 2: Ch 1, sc in first sc, [ch 1, sk next sc, sc in each of next 3 sc] 7 times, ch 1, sk next sc, sc in last sc. *(23 sc, 8 ch-1 sps)*

Row 3: Ch 1, sc in first sc, [ch 1, sk next ch-1 sp, sc in each of next 3 sc] 7 times, ch 1, sk next sc, sc in last sc, change color to steel blue, turn.

Row 4: Ch 1, sc in first sc, [hdc in ch-1 sp 2 rows below, sc in each of next 3 sc] 7 times, hdc in last ch-1 sp 2 rows below, sc in last sc, turn. *(23 sc, 8 hdc)*

Row 5 (first dec row): Ch 1, sc in first 2 sts, **sc dec** *(see Stitch Guide)* in next 2 sts, [sc in next 2 sts, sc dec in next 2 sts] 6 times, sc in each of last 3 sc, change color to tan, turn. *(24 sc)*

Row 6: Ch 1, sc in first sc, [ch 1, sk next sc, sc in each of next 2 sc] 7 times, ch 1, sk next sc, sc in last sc, turn. *(16 sc, 8 ch-1 sps)*

Row 7: Ch 1, sc in first sc, [ch 1, sk next ch-1 sp, sc in each of next 2 sc] 7 times, ch 1, sk last ch-1 sp, sc in last sc, change color to steel blue, turn.

Row 8: Ch 1, sc in first sc, [hdc in next ch-1 sp 2 rows below, sc in each of next 2 sc] 7 times, hdc in last ch-1 sp 2 rows below, sc in last sc, turn. *(16 sc, 8 hdc)*

Row 9 (2nd dec row): Ch 1, sc in first sc, sc dec in next 2 sts, [sc in next st, sc dec in next 2 sts] 6 times, sc in each of last 3 sts, change color to tan, turn. *(17 sc)*

Row 10: Ch 1, sc in first sc, [ch 1, sk next sc, sc next sc] 8 times, turn. *(9 sc, 8 ch-1 sps)*

Row 11: Ch 1, sc in first sc, [ch 1, sk next ch-1 sp, sc in next sc] 8 times, change color to steel blue, turn.

Row 12: Ch 1, sc in first sc, [hdc in ch-1 sp 2 rows below, sc in next sc] 8 times, turn. *(9 sc, 8 hdc)*

Row 13 (3rd dec row): Ch 1, sc in first sc, [sc dec in next 2 sts] 8 times, change color to tan, turn. *(9 sc)*

Row 14: Ch 1, sc in first sc, [ch 1, sk next sc, sc in next sc] 4 times, turn. *(5 sc, 4 ch-1 sps)*

Row 15: Ch 1, sc in each sc across, change color to steel blue, turn. Cut B. *(5 sc)*

Row 16: Ch 1, sc in first sc, sc dec in next 3 sc, sc in last sc, turn.

Row 17: Do not ch 1, sc in first sc, sk next sc, sc in last sc. Fasten off. **Place marker** *(see Pattern Notes)* in sp between sc for placement of first st of Shells. *(2 sc)*

Row 2

Right Edge Half-Shell

Foundation row (RS): With RS of first Shell of previous row facing and working in ends of rows, **sc join** *(see Special Stitch)* steel blue in first row, evenly place 14 sc across row ends, turn. *(15 sc)*

Row 1: Ch 1, sc in each sc across, change color to tan, turn.

Row 2: Ch 1, sc in first sc, [ch 1, sk next sc, sc in each of next 3 sc] 3 times, ch 1, sk next sc, sc in last sc, turn. *(11 sc, 4 ch-1 sps)*

Row 3: Ch 1, sc in first sc, [ch 1, sk next ch-1 sp, sc in each of next 3 sc] 3 times, ch 1, sk last ch-1 sp, sc in last sc, change color to steel blue, turn.

Row 4: Ch 1, sc in first sc, [hdc in next ch-1 sp 2 rows below, sc in each of next 3 sc] 3 times, hdc in next ch-1 sp 2 rows below, sc in last sc, turn. *(11 sc, 4 hdc)*

Row 5 (first dec row): Ch 1, sc in first 2 sts, [sc dec in next 2 sc, sc in next 2 sts] 3 times, sc in last sc, change color to tan, turn. *(12 sc)*

Row 6: Ch 1, sc in first sc, [ch 1, sk next sc, sc in each of next 2 sc] 3 times, ch 1, sk next sc, sc in last sc, turn. *(8 sc, 4 ch-1 sps)*

Row 7: Ch 1, sc in first sc, [ch 1, sk next ch-1 sp, sc in each of next 2 sc] 3 times, ch 1, sk last ch-1 sp, sc in last sc, change color to steel blue, turn.

Row 8: Ch 1, sc in first sc, [hdc in next ch-1 sp 2 rows below, sc in each of next 2 sc] 3 times, hdc in next ch-1 sp 2 rows below, sc in last sc, turn. *(8 sc, 4 hdc)*

Row 9 (2nd dec row): Ch 1, sc in first sc, [sc dec in next 2 sts, sc in next st] 3 times, sc in each of last 2 sc, change color to tan, turn.

Row 10: Ch 1, sc in first sc, [ch 1, sk next sc, sc in next sc] 4 times, turn. *(5 sc, 4 ch-1 sps)*

Row 11: Ch 1, sc in first sc, [ch 1, sk next ch-1 sp, sc in next sc] 4 times, change color to steel blue, turn.

Row 12: Ch 1, sc in first sc, [hdc in next ch-1 sp 2 rows below, sc in next sc] 3 times, hdc in next ch-1 sp 2 rows below, sc in last sc, turn. *(5 sc, 4 hdc)*

Row 13 (3rd dec row): Ch 1, sc in first sc, [sc dec in next 2 sts] 4 times, change color to tan, turn. *(5 sc)*

Row 14: Ch 1, sc in first sc, [ch 1, sk next sc, sc in next sc] twice, turn. *(3 sc, 2 ch-1 sps)*

Row 15: Ch 1, sc in each sc across, change color to steel blue, turn. Cut tan. *(3 sc)*

Row 16: Ch 1, sc in each sc across, turn.

Row 17: Do not ch 1, sc in first sc, sk next sc, sc in last sc. Fasten off. Place marker in sp between sc. *(2 sc)*

First Shell

Foundation row: Sc join steel blue in left marked sp of Shell just worked over, working in ends of rows across left edge, sc in next 14 rows, sc dec in last row of same Shell and first row of next Shell to join adjacent corners, working in ends of rows of next Shell, evenly sp 14 sc across right edge to marked sp, sc in marked sp, turn. *(31 sc)*

Work rows 1–17 of Shell.

Next Shell
Make 4 [5, 6, 7, 8].

Beg in last Shell worked over and continuing in next Shell of previous row, rep First Shell.

Left Edge Half-Shell

Foundation row: Sc join steel blue in marked sp of last Shell worked over, working in ends of rows across left edge, evenly place 14 sc across row ends, turn. *(15 sc)*

Rep rows 1–17 of Half-Shell.

Row 3

First Shell
Beg in marked sp of Right Edge Half-Shell, work same as First Shell of Row 2.

Next Shell
Make 5 [6, 7, 8, 9].

Work same as Next Shell of Row 2.

Row 4
Rep Row 2. Do not remove markers of last 2 rows.

Row 5

First Fill-in Shell
Row 1 (RS): With RS facing, sc join steel blue in marked sp at top of Half-Shell, remove marker, working in ends of rows, evenly place 14 sc across row ends, sc in next marked sp, remove marker, working in ends of rows of next Shell, evenly place 14 sc across row ends, sc in next marked sp, remove marker, turn. *(31 sc)*

Row 2: Ch 1, sc dec in first 2 sc, sc in next 12 sc, sc dec in next 3 sc, sc in next 12 sc, sc dec in last 2 sc, turn. *(27 sc)*

Row 3: Ch 1, sc dec in first 2 sc, sc dec in next 2 sc, sc in next 8 sc, sc dec in next 3 sc, sc in next 8 sc, [sc dec in next 2 sc] twice, turn. *(21 sc)*

Row 4: Ch 1, sc dec in first 2 sc, sc dec in next 2 sc, sc in next 5 sc, sc dec in next 3 sc, sc in next 5 sc, [sc dec in next 2 sc] twice, turn. *(15 sc)*

Row 5: Ch 1, sc dec in first 2 sc, sc dec in next 2 sc, sc in next 2 sc, sc dec in next 3 sc, sc in next 2 sc, [sc dec in next 2 sc] twice, turn. *(9 sc)*

Row 6: Ch 1, sc dec in first 2 sc, sc dec in next 2 sc, sc in next sc, [sc dec in next 2 sc] twice, turn. *(5 sc)*

Row 7: Ch 1, sc dec in first 2 sc, sc in next sc, sc dec in last 2 sc, turn. *(3 sc)*

Row 8: Do not ch 1, sc dec in 3 sc. Fasten off. *(1 sc)*

Next Fill-in Shell
Make 5 [6, 7, 8, 9].

Row 1: Beg in next marked sp of Shell just worked over, rep Row 1 of First Fill-in Shell.

Rows 2–8: Rep rows 2–8 of First Fill-in Shell.

Yoke
Row 1: With RS facing, sc join steel blue in top point of Half Shell, [29 sc across top of Fill-in Shell, sc in Shell point] 5 [6, 7, 8, 9] times, turn. *(151 [181, 211, 241, 271] sc)*

Row 2: Ch 1, sc in each sc across, turn.

Right Front
Row 1: Ch 2 *(see Pattern Notes)*, dc in next sc, dc in next 35 [42, 50, 57, 65] sc, turn, leave rem sts unworked. *(36 [43, 51, 58, 66] dc)*

Row 2: Ch 2, dc in next dc, dc in each rem dc across, turn.

Rep row 2 until work measures 5½ [6, 6½, 7, 7½] inches from beg, ending last row at front edge.

Shape Neck
Row 1: Ch 1, sl st in first 10 [11, 12, 13, 14] dc, ch 2, dc in each rem dc across, turn. *(27 [33, 40, 46, 53] dc)*

Row 2: Ch 2, dc in next dc, dc in each dc to last 3 dc, **dc dec** *(see Stitch Guide)* in next 2 dc, dc in last dc, turn. *(26 [32, 39, 45, 52] dc)*

Row 3: Ch 2, dc dec in next 2 sts, dc in each rem dc across, turn. *(25 [31, 38, 44, 51] dc)*

Rows 4 & 5: Rep rows 2 and 3. *(23 [29, 36, 42, 49] dc)*

Fasten off.

Back
Row 1: With RS facing, sk 4 sc from Right Front, join steel blue in next sc, ch 2, dc in next 70 [86, 100, 116, 130] sc, turn, leave rem sts unworked. *(71 [87, 101, 117, 131] dc)*

Row 2: Ch 2, dc in next st, dc in each rem dc across, turn.

Rep row 2 until Back is 3 rows less than Right Front.

Shape Right Neck
Row 1: Ch 2, dc in next dc, dc in next 23 [29, 36, 42, 49] dc, turn, leaving rem sts unworked. *(25 [31, 38, 44, 51] dc)*

Row 2: Ch 2, dc dec in next 2 dc, dc in each rem dc to end, turn. *(24 [30, 37, 43, 50] dc)*

Row 3: Ch 2, dc in next dc, dc in each dc to last 3 dc, dc dec in next 2 dc, 1 dc in last dc. Fasten off. *(23 [29, 36, 42, 49] dc)*

Shape Left Neck
Row 1 (RS): Sk next *(center)* 21 [25, 25, 29, 29] sts, join steel blue in next dc, ch 2, dc in rem 24 [30, 37, 43, 50] dc, turn. *(25 [31, 38, 44, 51] dc)*

Row 2: Ch 2, dc in next dc, dc in each dc to last 3 dc, dc dec in next 2 dc, 1 dc in last dc. *(24 [30, 37, 43, 50] dc)*

Row 3: Ch 2, dc dec in next 2 dc, dc in each rem dc to end, turn. Fasten off. *(23 [29, 36, 42, 49] dc)*

Left Front
Row 1: With RS facing, sk 4 sc from Back, join steel blue in next sc, ch 2, dc in next sc, dc in each rem sc across, turn. *(36 [43, 51, 58, 66] dc)*

Row 2: Ch 2, dc in next dc, dc in each rem dc across, turn.

Rep row 2 until work measures 5½ [6, 6½, 7, 7½] inches from beg, ending last row at arm edge.

Shape Neck
Row 1: Ch 2, dc in next dc, dc in next 25 [31, 38, 44, 51] dc, turn, leaving rem 9 [10, 11, 12, 13] dc unworked. *(27 [33, 40, 46, 53] dc)*

Row 2: Ch 2, dc dec in next 2 sts, dc in each rem dc across, turn. *(26 [32, 39, 45, 52] dc)*

Row 3: Ch 2, dc in each dc to last 3 dc, dc dec in next 2 dc, dc in last dc, turn. *(25 [31, 38, 44, 51] dc)*

Rows 4 & 5: Rep rows 2 and 3. *(23 [29, 36, 42, 49] dc)*

Fasten off.

Sleeve
Make 2.

Cuff
Row 1: With G hook and steel blue, ch 15. Starting in 2nd ch from hook, sc in each rem ch across, turn. *(14 sc)*

Row 2: Ch 1, working in **back lps** *(see Stitch Guide)*, sc in first sc and each rem sc across, turn.

Rep row 2 until there are a total of 30 [32, 34, 36, 38] rows. Do not fasten off, do not turn at end of last row.

Arm
Rotate Cuff to work along row ends. Mark this as RS of work.

Row 1: Ch 1, 2 sc in first row end, *1 sc in next row end, 2 sc in next row end, rep from * to last row end, sc in last row end, turn. *(45 [48, 51, 54, 57] sc)*

Row 2: Ch 3, dc in next sc, 2 dc in next sc *(inc made)*, [dc in each of next 2 sc, 2 dc in next sc] 14 [15, 16, 17, 18] times, turn. *(60 [64, 68, 72, 76] dc)*

Row 3: Ch 3, dc in next and each rem dc, turn.

Rep row 3 until sleeve measures 2 inches from end of cuff, ending with a WS row.

Next inc row: Ch 3, 2 dc in next dc, dc across to last 2 dc, 2 dc in next dc, dc in last dc, turn. *(62 [66, 70, 74, 78] dc)*

[Rep row 3 until sleeve measures 2 inches from last inc row. Rep inc row] 3 times. *(68 [72, 76, 80, 84] dc)*

Rep row 3 until sleeve measures 18 inches from beg for all sizes. Fasten off.

Finishing

Sew Shoulder seams. Fold Sleeves in half, mark center top of sleeve, pin sleeve in place matching center of sleeve with shoulder seam, side of sleeve cap with yoke of cardi, sew in place. Sew underarm seams.

Front & Neck Borders

Row 1 (RS): Join steel blue in top of Shell at bottom Right Front, evenly place 16 sc across row edges of first Half Shell, evenly place 16 sc across row edges of next Half Shell, evenly place 19 [21, 23, 25, 27] sc across yoke to last row end, 3 sc in last row end *(corner made, place marker in center sc)*, rotate to work across neck shaping, sc in next 9 [10, 11, 12, 13] sts, evenly place 10 sc across Right Front shaping, evenly place 5 sc along Right Back shaping, sc in next 21 [25, 25, 29, 29] sts along Back, evenly place 5 sc along Left Back shaping, evenly place 10 sc along Left Front shaping, sc in next 9 [10, 11, 12, 13] sts, rotate to work across Left Front, 3 sc in first row end *(corner made, place marker in center sc)*, evenly place 19 [21, 23, 25, 27] sc across row ends of Yoke, [evenly place 16 sc in next Half Shell] twice, do not turn. Do not fasten off steel blue.

Row 2 (RS): Sc join tan in first sc at Bottom Right, [sc in each sc to next marked sc, 3 sc in marked sc] twice, sc in each sc to end, pick up a lp of steel blue, turn. Fasten off tan.

Row 3: Ch 1, [sc in each sc to next marked sc, 3 sc in marked sc] twice, sc in each sc to last 2 sc before end of yoke on Right Front, ch 3, sk 2 sc *(buttonhole made)*, sc in each rem sc to end. Fasten off.

Sew button on Left Front opposite buttonhole, fold back top of fronts to form lapels.

Blocking

Place garment on a padded surface, sprinkle lightly with water, pat into shape, pin, being sure to use rustproof pins, allow to dry. ●

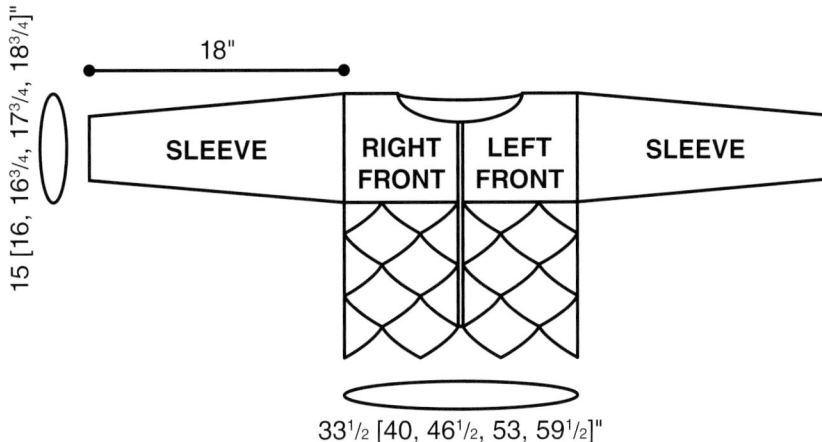

15 [16, 16¾, 17¾, 18¾]"

18"

SLEEVE RIGHT FRONT LEFT FRONT SLEEVE

33½ [40, 46½, 53, 59½]"

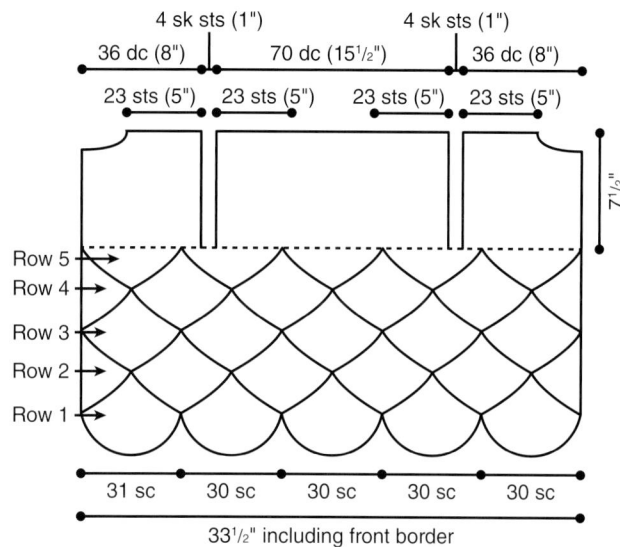

Captivating Cardi
Placement Diagram Size Small
Note:
Row 1—5 individual shells
Rows 2 & 4—4 shells & ¹/₂ shell each side
Row 3—5 shells

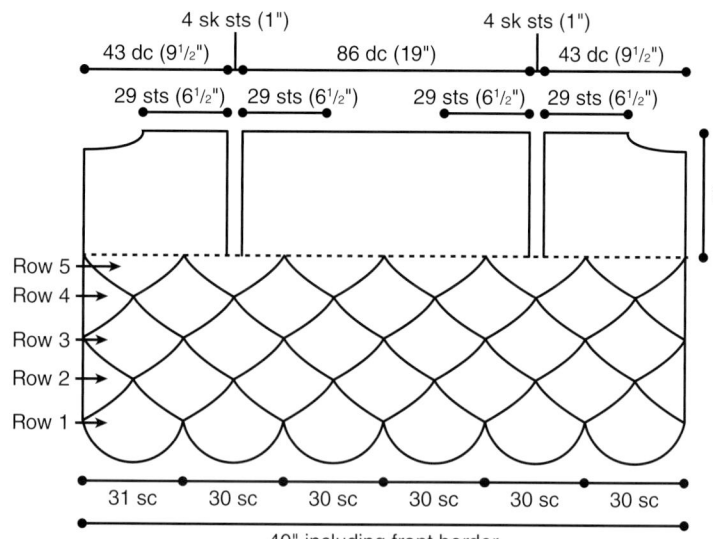

Captivating Cardi
Placement Diagram Size Medium
Note:
Row 1—6 individual shells
Rows 2 & 4—5 shells & ¹/₂ shell each side
Row 3—6 shells

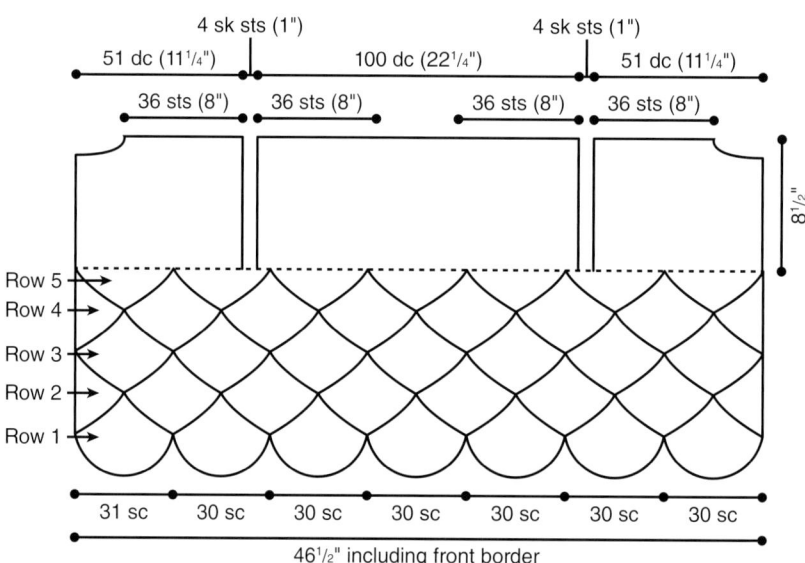

Captivating Cardi
Placement Diagram Size Large
Note:
Row 1—7 individual shells
Rows 2 & 4—6 shells & ¹/₂ shell each side
Row 3—7 shells

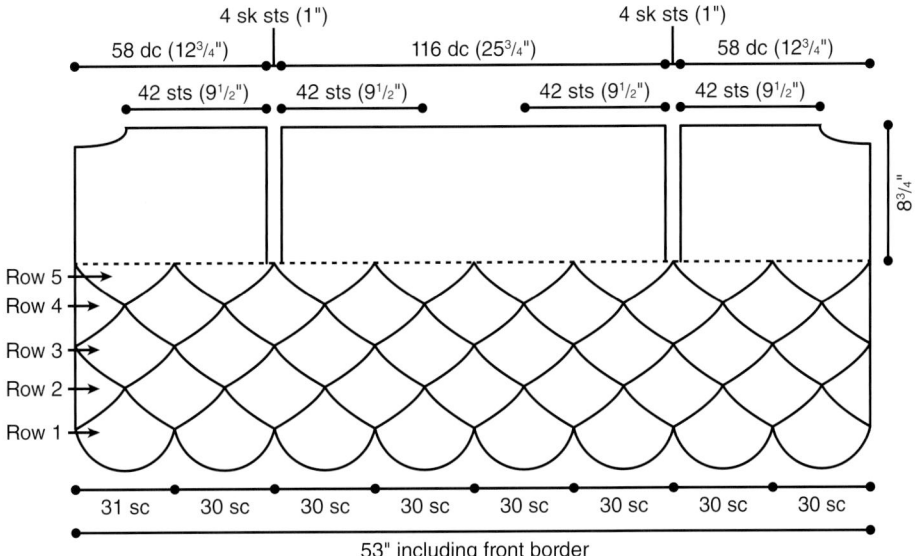

Captivating Cardi
Placement Diagram Size X-Large
Note:
Row 1—8 individual shells
Rows 2 & 4—7 shells & ¹/₂ shell each side
Row 3—8 shells

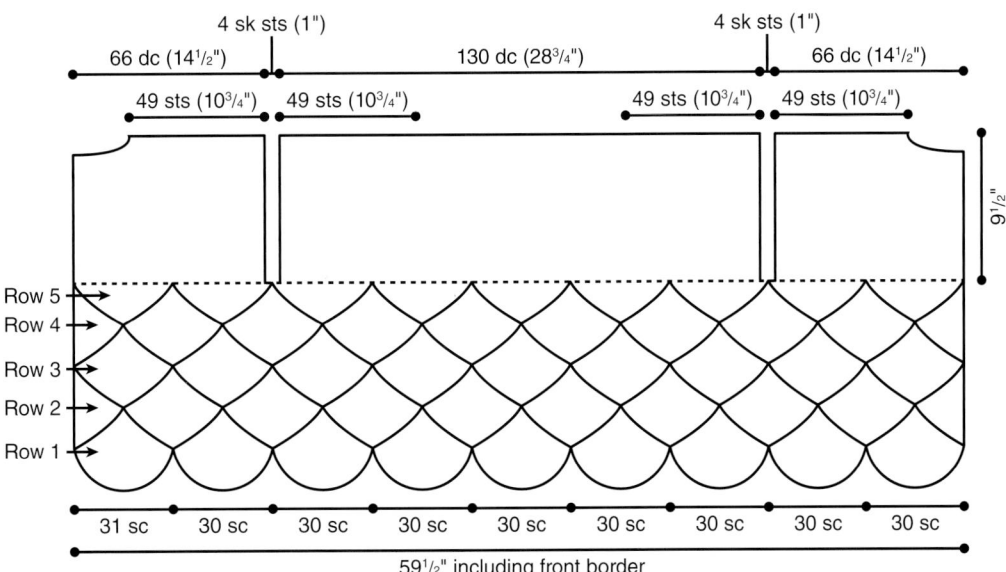

Captivating Cardi
Placement Diagram Size 2X-Large
Note:
Row 1—9 individual shells
Rows 2 & 4—8 shells & ¹/₂ shell each side
Row 3—9 shells

Color Me Autumn Vest

Skill Level
 INTERMEDIATE

Finished Sizes
Instructions given fit woman's size small; changes for medium, large, X-large and 2X-large are in [ ].

Finished Measurement
Bust: 37½ inches *(small)* [40 inches *(medium)*, 42½ inches *(large)*, 52½ inches *(X-large)*, 56 inches *(2X-large)*]

Materials

- Premier Yarns Basix DK light (DK) weight acrylic yarn (3½ oz/ 306 yds/100g per ball):
  - 4 [4, 5, 6, 6] balls #1142-42 mocha
  - 2 [2, 2, 2, 2] balls #1142-09 tangerine
- Premier Yarns Sweet Roll DK light (DK) weight acrylic yarn (5 oz/541 yds/140g per ball):
  - 1 [1, 1, 2, 2] ball(s) #2005-12 agate
- **Sizes small and X-large:** Size F/5/3.75mm crochet hook or size needed to obtain gauge
- **Sizes medium and 2X-large:** Size G/6/4mm crochet hook or size needed to obtain gauge
- **Size large:** Size 7/4.5mm crochet hook or size needed to obtain gauge
- 1-inch buttons: 6
- Stitch markers: 2
- Tapestry needle
- Rustproof pins

Gauge
Small: Each square measures 3¾ inches, 16 sc = 3¾ inches with size F/5 hook

Medium: Each square measures 4 inches, 16 sc = 4 inches with size G/6 hook

Large: Each square measures 4¼ inches, 16 sc = 4¼ inches with size 7 hook

X-large: Each square measures 3¾ inches, 16 sc = 3¾ inches with size F/5 hook

2X-large: Each square measures 4 inches, 16 sc = 4 inches with size G/6 hook

Take time to check gauge.

Pattern Notes
Before stitching begins, see Pattern Notes on page 3.

Vest is made in one piece up to armholes then divided for Fronts and Back.

Weave in loose ends as work progresses.

Entire vest is worked using designated hook for size being made.

Vest is made using both Textured Squares *(see instructions on page 4)* and 2-Color Squares *(see instructions on page 3)*, working all stitches in back loops unless otherwise stated.

When working along row ends, work 1 single crochet in each row end.

Join with slip stitch as indicated unless otherwise stated.

Vest

Tier 1

First Square
With mocha and beg at bottom right front *(see Layout Diagram)* work **Textured Square** *(see Pattern Notes)*. Do not fasten off, do not turn.

2nd Square
With mocha, work 16 sc **along side of square** *(see Pattern Notes)* just completed, ch 18, turn, complete Textured Square. Fasten off after last square.

3rd–10th [3rd–10th, 3rd–10th, 3rd–14th, 3rd–14th] Squares

Continuing with mocha, work all rem squares same as 2nd square.

Tier 2

First Square

With mocha and beg at left front, ch 17, **join** *(see Pattern Notes)* at top of last square made in tier below, work 16 sc along top of this square, *(beg ch-17 and 16 sc count as foundation row)*, turn.

Work rows 1–16 of 2-Color Square alternating mocha and tangerine. Fasten off.

2nd Square

Join mocha at top right corner of next square from tier below, work 16 sc along top of this square, 1 sc in corner then 16 sc along side of first square, turn, complete 2-Color Square alternating mocha and tangerine.

3rd–10th [3rd–10th, 3rd–10th, 3rd–14th, 3rd–14th] Squares

Work all rem squares same as 2nd square.

Tier 3

First Square

With agate throughout and beg at right side, ch 17, join at top of last square made on Tier 2, work 16 sc along top of this square, turn, complete Textured Square.

Fasten off.

2nd–10th [2nd–10th, 2nd–10th, 2nd–14th, 2nd–14th] Squares

Join agate at top of square just completed, work 16 sc along side of this square, 1 sc in corner then 16 sc along top of next square from tier below, turn, complete Textured Square with agate throughout.

Tier 4

Rep Tier 2.

Right Front Armhole Shaping

Armhole Shaping consists of only two rows of 2 [2, 2, 3, 3] squares each.

Tier 1

First Square

With mocha throughout and beg at right side, ch 17, join at top of last square made on tier below, work 16 sc along top of square, turn, complete Textured Square. Fasten off.

2nd [2nd, 2nd, 2nd & 3rd, 2nd & 3rd] Square(s)

Join mocha at top of square just completed, work 16 sc along side of this square, 1 sc in corner then 16 sc along top of next square from tier below, turn, complete Textured Square *(2 squares made)*. Fasten off. Right front armhole shaping complete for Small, Medium and Large; make 1 more square for X-large and 2X-large.

Tier 2

First Square

With mocha, ch 17, join at top of square just completed, work 16 sc along top of square, turn, complete 2-Color Square alternating mocha and tangerine. Fasten off.

2nd [2nd, 2nd, 2nd & 3rd, 2nd & 3rd] Square(s)

Join mocha at top of First Square, work 16 sc along side of this square, 1 sc in corner then 16 sc along top of next square from tier below, turn, complete 2-Color Square alternating mocha and tangerine. Fasten off. Right front armhole shaping complete for Small, Medium and Large; make 1 more square for X-large and 2X-large.

Left Front Armhole Shaping

Sk 6 [6, 6, 8, 8] squares in center, work on rem 2 [2, 2, 3, 3] squares on Left Front as follows.

Tier 1

First Square

With mocha throughout, ch 17, join at top of 2nd square in from front edge on tier below, work 16 sc along top of square, turn, complete Textured Square. Fasten off.

2nd [2nd, 2nd, 2nd & 3rd, 2nd & 3rd] Square(s)

Rep 2nd [2nd, 2nd, 2nd and 3rd, 2nd and 3rd] Squares of Right Front Armhole Shaping Tier 1.

Tier 2

Rep all squares from Tier 2 of Right Front Armhole Shaping.

Top Back

Tier 1

First Square

With mocha, sk 1 square from Right Front Armhole Shaping *(for armhole)*, ch 17, join at top of next square on tier below, work 16 sc along top of square, turn, complete Textured Square. Fasten off.

2nd Square

Join mocha at top of square just completed, work 16 sc along side of this square, 1 sc in corner then 16 sc along top of next square from tier below, turn, complete Textured Square with mocha throughout. Fasten off.

3rd–4th [3rd–4th, 3rd–4th, 3rd–6th, 3rd–6th] Squares

Continuing with mocha, work all rem squares same as 2nd square.

Tier 2

First Square

With mocha, ch 17, join at top of last square made on tier below, work 16 sc along top of square, turn, complete 2-Color Square alternating mocha and tangerine. Fasten off.

2nd Square

Join mocha at top of Square just completed, work 16 sc along side of this square, 1 sc in corner then 16 sc along top of next square from tier below, turn, complete 2-Color Square alternating mocha and tangerine. Fasten off.

3rd–4th [3rd–4th, 3rd–4th, 3rd–6th, 3rd–6th] Squares

Work all rem squares same as 2nd square.

Back Shoulder Shaping

Row 1: With RS facing, join agate at top of first square on Back, ch 1, work 16 sc across each of 4 [4, 4, 6, 6] squares, turn. *(64 [64, 64, 96, 96] sc)*

Left Shoulder Shaping

Row 2 (WS): Beg left shoulder shaping, ch 1, sc in first 13 sc, **sc dec** (see Stitch Guide) in next 2 sc, sc in next sc, turn, leaving rem sts unworked. *(15 sc)*

Row 3: Ch 1, sc in first sc, sc dec in next 2 sc, sc in next 12 sc, turn. *(14 sc)*

Row 4: Ch 1, sc in first 11 sc, sc dec in next 2 sc, sc in last sc, turn. *(13 sc)*

Row 5: Ch 1, sc in first sc, sc dec in next 2 sc, sc in next 10 sc, turn. *(12 sc)*

Rows 6 & 7: Ch 1, sc in each sc across, turn.

[Rep rows 6 and 7] 0 [0, 1, 2, 2] time(s).

Fasten off.

Right Shoulder Shaping

Row 1 is already done on this side.

Row 2: Sk center unworked 32 [32, 32, 64, 64] sc on row 1, join agate in next sc, ch 1, sc in same sc as join, sc dec in next 2 sc, sc in next 13 sc, turn. *(15 sc)*

Row 3: Ch 1, sc in first 12 sc, sc dec in next 2 sc, sc in next sc, turn. *(14 sc)*

Row 4: Ch 1, sc in first sc, sc dec in next 2 sc, sc in next 11 sc, turn. *(13 sc)*

Row 5: Ch 1, sc in first 10 sc, sc dec in next 2 sc, sc in last sc, turn. *(12 sc)*

Rows 6 & 7: Ch 1, sc in each sc across, turn.

[Rep rows 6 and 7] 0 [0, 1, 2, 2] time(s).

Fasten off.

Right Front Shoulder Shaping

Row 1: Join agate at front edge with RS facing, ch 1, work 16 sc across each of 2 [2, 2, 3, 3] squares, turn. *(32 [32, 32, 48, 48] sc)*

Row 2 (WS): Ch 1, sc in first 13 sc, sc dec in next 2 sc, sc in last sc, turn, leaving rem 16 [16, 16, 32, 32] sc unworked. *(15 sc)*

Row 3: Ch 1, sc in first sc, sc dec in next 2 sc, sc in next 12 sc, turn. *(14 sc)*

Row 4: Ch 1, 1 sc in first 11 sc, sc dec in next 2 sc, sc in last sc, turn. *(13 sc)*

Row 5: Ch 1, sc in first sc, sc dec in next 2 sc, sc in next 10 sc, turn. *(12 sc)*

Rows 6 & 7: Ch 1, sc in each sc across, turn.

Fasten off.

Left Front Shoulder Shaping

Row 1: Join agate at armhole edge with RS facing, work 16 sc across each of 2 [2, 2, 3, 3] squares, turn. *(32 [32, 32, 48, 48] sc)*

Row 2 (WS): Sl st in first 16 sc, ch 1, sc in next sc, sc dec in next 2 sc, sc in next 13 sc, turn. *(15 sc)*

Row 3: Ch 1, sc in first 12 sc, sc dec in next 2 sc, sc next sc, turn. *(14 sc)*

Row 4: Ch 1, sc in first sc, sc dec in next 2 sc, sc in next 11 sc, turn. *(13 sc)*

Row 5: Ch 1, sc in first 10 sc, sc dec in next 2 sc, sc in last sc, turn. *(12 sc)*

Rows 6 & 7: Ch 1, sc in each sc across, turn.

[Rep rows 6 and 7] 0 [0, 1, 2, 2] time(s).

Fasten off.

Finishing

Sew Shoulder seams.

Front & Neck Border

Sizes Small, Medium & Large Only

Row 1: With mocha, starting at bottom Right Front, work 16 sc across side of each square to corner, work 2 more sc in last st to turn corner, place marker in center of 3 sts to mark corner, sk 1 sc, work 15 sc along top of first square, work 7 [7, 9] sc along side of Right Front Shoulder Shaping, 7 [7, 9] sc along Back Shoulder Shaping, 32 sc along back neck, 7 [7, 9] sc along Back Shoulder Shaping, 7 [7, 9] sc along Left Front Shoulder Shaping, 15 sc along top of next square, sk 1 sc, work 3 sc in top corner st of left side, place marker in center of 3 sts to mark corner, 15 sc in rem sts of first square, 16 sc across each square to bottom left. Fasten off.

Sizes X-large & 2X-large Only

[Row 1]: With mocha, starting at bottom Right Front, work 16 sc in across side of each square to corner,

work 2 more sc in last st to turn corner, place marker in center of 3 sts to mark corner, sk 1 sc, work 15 sc along top of first square, work 16 sc across 2nd square, work [11, 11] sc along side of Right Front Shoulder Shaping, [11, 11] sc along Back Shoulder Shaping, 64 sc along back neck, [11, 11] sc along Back Shoulder Shaping, [11, 11] sc along Front Shoulder Shaping, 16 sc along top of next square, 15 sc along top next square, sk 1 sc, work 3 sc in top corner st of left side, place marker in center of 3 sts to mark corner, 15 sc in rem sts of first square, 16 sc across each square to bottom left. Fasten off.

All Sizes

Row 2: Join agate in first sc of row 1, [sc in each sc to marked st, 3 sc in marked st] twice, sc in each sc to bottom of Left Front, turn. Move markers to center corner st and continue to move up as work progresses.

Row 3 (buttonhole row): [Sc in each sc to marked st, 3 sc in marked st] twice, *ch 3, sk 3 sc, sc in each of next 13 sc, rep from * 5 times *(6 buttonholes made)*, sc to end of row, turn.

Row 4: Sc across by working sc in each sc, 3 sc in each ch-3 sp and 3 sc in each corner st. Fasten off.

Row 5: Join mocha in bottom right corner, [sc in each sc to marked st, 3 sc in marked st] twice, sc to end of row. Fasten off.

Armhole Borders

Row 1: Starting at center of armhole square on Left Front, join mocha, ch 1, work 8 sc along top of square, [16 sc along side of next Back square] twice, 7 [7, 9, 11, 11] sc along Back Shoulder Shaping, 7 [7, 9, 11, 11] along Front Shoulder Shaping, [16 sc along next Front square] twice, 8 sc along underarm square, join to first ch-1, do not fasten off mocha, draw up a loop with agate, do not turn.

Row 2: With agate, ch 1, sc in each sc around, join to beg ch-1, do not turn.

Rows 3 & 4: [Rep row 2] twice.

Row 5: Pick up lp of mocha, fasten off agate, rep row 2. Fasten off.

Rep for Right Armhole.

Sew buttons opposite buttonholes on Left Front.

Blocking

Place garment on a padded surface, sprinkle lightly with water, pat gently into shape, pin using rustproof pins and allow to dry. ●

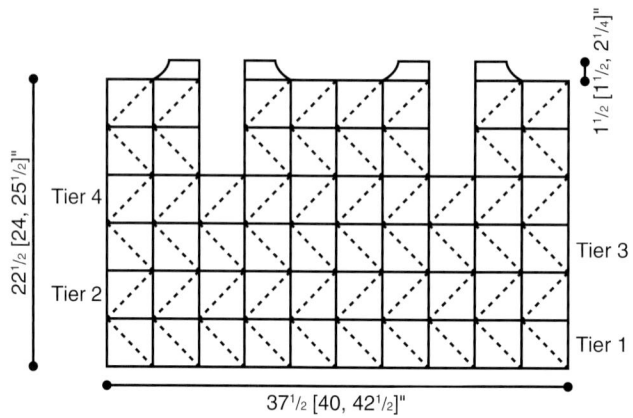

Color Me Autumn Vest
Layout Diagram
Sizes Small, Medium & Large

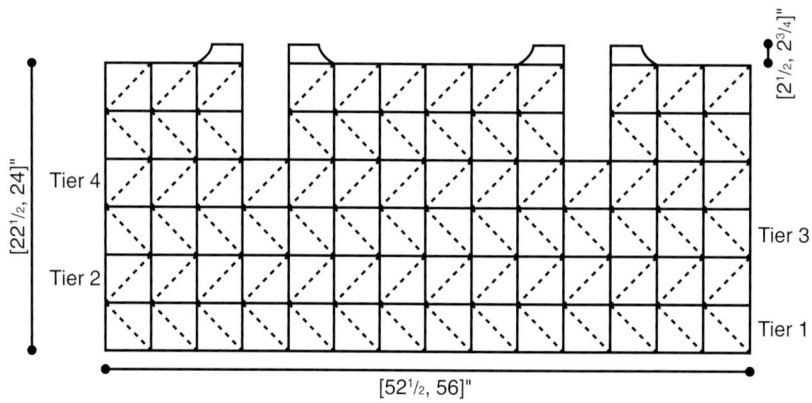

Color Me Autumn Vest
Layout Diagram
Sizes X-Large & 2X-Large

Beanie Squared

Skill Level

 **INTERMEDIATE**

Finished Measurements

20 inches in circumference x 9 inches tall

Materials

- Premier Yarns Basix DK light (DK) weight acrylic yarn (3½ oz/ 360 yds/100g per ball):
    1 ball #1142-42 mocha
- Premier Yarns Sweet Roll DK light (DK) weight acrylic yarn (5 oz/541 yds/140g per ball):
    1 ball #2005-12 agate
- Size G/6/4mm crochet hook or size needed to obtain gauge
- Tapestry needle
- Stitch marker
- 3-inch piece of heavy cardboard

Gauge

Square = 4 inches square

Pattern Notes

Before stitching begins, see Pattern Notes on page 3.

Beanie is made with 2-Color Squares *(see instructions on page 3)*, working all stitches in back loops unless otherwise stated.

Colors change at end of every odd-numbered row. Do not fasten off after each color change; carry yarn not in use up sides, twisting new color with last color worked.

Weave in loose ends as work progresses.

Chain-1 at beginning or end of row or round does not count as a stitch unless otherwise stated.

When building Squares, always join with right side facing.

Refer to Assembly Diagram for order of Squares and where to join new Squares.

Beginning chains will be either 16 or 17 chains, depending on the placement of chains at the beginning or end of indicated row. When working next row of single crochet in beginning chains, always work in **back bar of chains** *(see illustration on page 3)*.

Join with slip stitch as indicated unless otherwise stated.

Beanie

Tier 1

First Square

Beg with mocha, work **2-Color Square** *(see Pattern Notes)*. At end of last row, fasten off.

2nd–5th Squares

With mocha, **ch 17** *(see Pattern Notes)*, **join** *(see Assembly Diagram and Pattern Notes)* at bottom right corner of last square made, sc in end of each row of previous Square made *(beg ch-17 and 16 sc count as foundation row)*, turn. Work rows 1–16 of Square.

Tier 2

First Square

Working on top of Tier 1, join mocha at top right corner of First Square, work 17 sc evenly across top of First Square, ch 17 *(17 sc ch-17 count as foundation row)*, turn. Work rows 1–16 of Square.

2nd–5th Squares

Join mocha at top right corner of next square of Tier 1, work 16 sc evenly across top of same square, sc in corner between current Square and last Square worked, sc in end of each row of last square made, turn.

Work rows 1–16 of Square.

You now have 2 Tiers of 5 squares each. Sew seam to form a cylinder.

Top Shaping

Note: Work in both lps of each st throughout.

Rnd 1: Join mocha in top right corner of any Square, ch 1, work 10 sc evenly across top of each square around, join in beg ch-1. Do not turn, place marker in first sc. *(50 sc)*

Rnd 2: Ch 1, sc in first 2 sc, [sc dec in next 2 sc, sc in next sc] around, join in beg ch-1. *(34 sc)*

Rnd 3: Ch 1, sc in first 2 sc, [sc dec in next 2 sc, sc in next sc] around to last sc, sc in last sc, join in beg ch-1. *(23 sc)*

Rnd 4: Ch 1, sc in next sc, [sc dec in next 2 sc] 11 times, join in beg ch-1. Fasten off, leaving 10-inch tail. *(12 sc)*

Thread tail on tapestry needle, weave through sts of rnd 4 and pull gently to close crown. Fasten securely.

Bottom Border

Note: Work in both lps of each st throughout.

Rnd 1: With RS of bottom edge facing, join mocha in corner of any square, ch 1, work 16 sc evenly across each square, join in beg ch-1. *(80 sc)*

Rnds 2 & 3: Ch 1, sc in each sc around, join in beg ch-1.

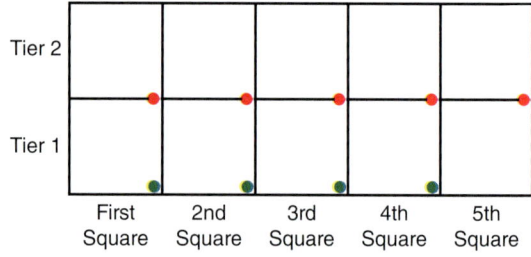

Beanie Squared
Assembly Diagram

KEY
● Join next Tier 1 Square here
● Join next Tier 2 Square here

Continued on page 39

Let's Go to the Market Bag

Skill Level

 INTERMEDIATE

Finished Measurements

28 inches in circumference x 16 inches tall, excluding Straps

Materials

- Premier Yarns Cotton Sprout light (DK) weight cotton yarn (3½ oz/230 yds/100g per ball):
  - 3 balls #1149-14 teal (A)
  - 2 balls #1149-15 turquoise (B)
  - 1 ball #1149-16 aqua (C)
- Size G/6/4/mm crochet hook or size needed to obtain gauge
- Tapestry needle

Gauge

Square: 4 inches square; 5½ inches across diagonal

Pattern Notes

Before stitching begins, see Pattern Notes on page 3.

Bag is made with Textured Squares *(see instructions on page 4)*, working all stitches in back loops unless otherwise stated.

Weave in loose ends as work progresses.

Join with slip stitch as indicated unless otherwise stated.

Beginning chains of 2nd Squares will be either 17 or 18 chains, depending on the placement of chains at the beginning or end of indicated row. When working next row of single crochet in beginning chains, always work in **back bar of chains** *(see illustration on page 3)*.

In Tier 4, do not fasten off color after each row; carry yarn not in use up sides, twisting new color with last color worked.

Refer to Assembly Diagram for position of Squares, joining beginning chains and sewing instructions.

Special Stitch

Single crochet join (sc join): Place a slip knot on hook, insert hook in indicated st, yo, pull up a lp, yo and draw through both lps on hook.

Bag

First Tier

Make 5.

With teal, **Textured Squares** *(see Pattern Notes)*.

Tier 2

Arrange squares with points as shown in Tier 1 of **Assembly Diagram** *(see Pattern Notes and Assembly Diagram)*.

First Square

Join *(see Pattern Notes)* turquoise at top point of First Square, ch 1, working across left edge, sc in end of each row *(16 sc)*, ch 1 *(counts as a st in next row)*, working across right edge of next Square, sc in end of each row *(16 sc)*, turn. Work rows 1–16 of Square.

2nd, 3rd and 4th Squares

Join turquoise at top of square just worked, rep First Square of Tier 2.

5th Square

Join turquoise at top of 5th square, working across left edge, ch 1, sc in end of each row *(16 sc)*, ch 18 *(16 sc and 18 chs count as foundation row)*, turn. Work rows 1–16 of Square.

Tier 3

First Square

With aqua, ch 17, working in ends of rows of First Square of Tier 2, join in first row *(see Diagram)*, working across right edge of Square, sc in each row *(16 sc)*, turn. Work rows 1–16 of Square.

2nd–5th Squares

Join aqua at top point of last Square worked of Tier 2, working across left edge, sc in end of each row *(16 sc)*, sc in top point of Square directly below in Tier 1, working across right edge of next Square, sc in end of each row *(16 sc)*, turn. Work rows 1–16 of Square.

Tier 4

Beg with teal, rep Tier 2, **changing color** *(see Stitch Guide and Pattern Notes)* in each Square in sequence of turquoise, aqua and teal at end of every odd-numbered row.

Tier 5

First Square

With teal and working in Squares of Tier 4, rep Tier 3.

Assembly

Referring to Assembly Diagram, bring side edges around, placing outer points between Tiers, sew tog to form a cylinder. In Tier 1, sew diagonal edges of adjacent Squares tog.

Half-Square
Make 5.

Row 1: With RS facing and working in ends of rows, **sc join** *(see Special Stitch)* teal in first row at top of any Square in Tier 5, ch 1, sc in next 14 rows, sc dec in next row, join between Squares and first row of next Square, working in ends of rows of next Square, sc in each rem row.

Rows 2–8: Rep rows 2–8 of Square. At end of last row, fasten off.

Top Border

Rnd 1: Join teal in top point of any Square, ch 1, sc in same point, [working in next Half-Square, sc in ends of first 8 rows, sc in next 5 sc, sc in ends of next 8 rows*, sc in point of next Square] around, ending last rep at *, join in beg ch-1. *(110 sc)*

Rnds 2–5: Ch 1, sc in each sc around, join in beg ch-1. At end of last rnd, turn, do not fasten off.

First Strap

Row 1: Ch 1, sc in each of next 18 sc, leave rem sc unworked, turn. *(18 sc)*

Row 2: Ch 1, sc in each sc across, turn.

Row 3: Ch 1, sc in first sc, sc dec in next 2 sc, sc in each sc across to last 3 sc, sc dec in next 2 sc, sc last sc, turn. *(16 sc)*

Rep rows 2 and 3 until 6 sts rem, then work even until Strap is 25 inches from beg.

Last row: Ch 1, sc dec in first 2 sc, sc in next 2 sc, sc dec in last 2 sts. Fasten off.

2nd Strap

Row 1: Sk next 37 sc, sc join teal in next sc, sc in next 17 sc, leave rem sc unworked, turn.

Beg with row 2, work same as First Strap.

Finishing

Blocking is not recommended for this bag.

Tie Straps tog to achieve desired length. ●

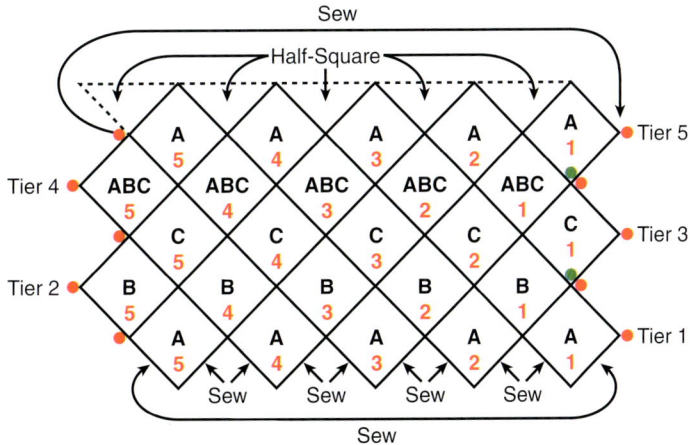

Let's Go to the Market Bag
Assembly Diagram

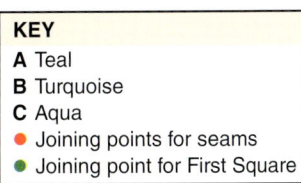

KEY
A Teal
B Turquoise
C Aqua
● Joining points for seams
● Joining point for First Square

Slouchy Shell Beanie

Skill Level

■■■□ INTERMEDIATE

Finished Measurements

Headband: 19 inches in circumference

Body: 24 inches in circumference

Height: 9 inches tall

Materials

- Premier Yarns Anti-Pilling Everyday DK light (DK) weight acrylic yarn (3½ oz/273 yds/100g per ball):
    1 ball each #1107-27 dove and #1107-56 mustard
- Size G/6/4mm crochet hook or size needed to obtain gauge
- Tapestry needle
- Stitch markers

Gauge

Shell: 6 inches wide x 4 inches long

Pattern Notes

Before stitching begins, see Pattern Notes on page 3.

Beanie is made of Shells worked with a join-as-you-go technique. Lower edge is finished with Fill-in Shells and Headband.

Except in Fill-in Shells, colors change at end of every odd-numbered row. Do not fasten off after each color change; carry yarn not in use up sides, twisting new color with last color worked.

Refer to Assembly Diagram for placement of Shells and marked stitches.

Weave in loose ends as work progresses.

Place markers where indicated and remove them as work progresses unless otherwise stated.

Join with slip stitch as indicated unless otherwise stated.

Special Stitch

Single crochet join (sc join): Place a slip knot on hook, insert hook in indicated st, yo, pull up a lp, yo and draw through both lps on hook.

Beanie

Rnd 1

Shell

Make 4.

Foundation row: With dove, ch 32.

Row 1 (WS): Working in **back bars of chs** *(see illustration on page 3)*, sc in 2nd ch from hook and in each ch across, **change color** *(see Stitch Guide and Pattern Notes)* to mustard, turn. *(31 sc)*

Row 2: Ch 1, sc in first sc, [ch 1, sk next sc, sc in each of next 3 sc] 7 times, ch 1, sk next sc, sc in last sc. *(23 sc, 8 ch-1 sps)*

Row 3: Ch 1, sc in first sc, [ch 1, sk next ch-1 sp, sc in each of next 3 sc] 7 times, ch 1, sk next sc, sc in last sc, change color to dove, turn.

Row 4: Ch 1, sc in first sc, [hdc in ch-1 sp 2 rows below, sc in each of next 3 sc] 7 times, hdc in last ch-1 sp 2 rows below, sc in last sc, turn. *(23 sc, 8 hdc)*

Row 5 (first dec row): Ch 1, sc in first 2 sts, **sc dec** *(see Stitch Guide)* in next 2 sts, [sc in next 2 sts, sc dec in next 2 sts] 6 times, sc in each of last 3 sts, change color to mustard, turn. *(24 sc)*

Row 6: Ch 1, sc in first sc, [ch 1, sk next sc, sc in each of next 2 sc] 7 times, ch 1, sk next sc, sc in last sc, turn. *(16 sc, 8 ch-1 sps)*

Row 7: Ch 1, sc in first sc, [ch 1, sk next ch-1 sp, sc in each of next 2 sc] 7 times, ch 1, sk last ch-1 sp, sc in last sc, change color to dove, turn.

Row 8: Ch 1, sc in first sc, [hdc in next ch-1 sp 2 rows below, sc in each of next 2 sc] 7 times, hdc in last ch-1 sp 2 rows below, sc in last sc, turn. *(16 sc, 8 hdc)*

Row 9 (2nd dec row): Ch 1, sc in first st, sc dec in next 2 sts, [sc in next st, sc dec in next 2 sts] 6 times, sc in each of last 3 sts, change color to mustard, turn. *(17 sc)*

Row 10: Ch 1, sc in first sc, [ch 1, sk next sc, sc next sc] 8 times, turn. *(9 sc, 8 ch-1 sps)*

Row 11: Ch 1, sc in first sc, [ch 1, sk next ch-1 sp, sc in next sc] 8 times, change color to dove, turn.

Row 12: Ch 1, sc in first sc, [hdc in ch-1 sp 2 rows below, sc in next sc] 8 times, turn. *(9 sc, 8 hdc)*

Row 13 (3rd dec row): Ch 1, sc in first sc, [sc dec in next 2 sts] 8 times, change color to mustard, turn. *(9 sc)*

Row 14: Ch 1, sc in first sc, [ch 1, sk next sc, sc in next sc] 4 times, turn. *(5 sc, 4 ch-1 sps)*

Row 15: Ch 1, sc in each sc across, change color to dove, turn. Cut mustard. *(5 sc)*

Row 16: Ch 1, sc in first sc, sc dec in next 3 sc, sc in last sc, turn.

Row 17: Do not ch 1, sc in first sc, sk next sc, sc in last sc. Fasten off. **Place marker** *(see Pattern Notes)* in sp between sc. *(2 sc)*

Rnd 2

Note: *Refer to Assembly Diagram for correct placement of Shells and joining sts.*

First Shell

Foundation row: With dove, ch 16, working in right edge of any Shell, sc in end of first 15 rows, turn. *(31 sc)*

Work rows 1–17 of Shell.

Next Shell
Make 3.

Foundation row: Working in left edge of same Shell, **sc join** *(see Special Stitch)* dove in end of first row, sc in ends of next 14 rows, ch 1 *(counts as st in next row)*, working in right edge of next Shell, sc in end of first 15 rows, turn. *(31 sc)*

Work rows 1–17 of Shell.

Rnd 3

Shell
Make 4.

Work same as Next Shell of Rnd 2.

Lower Edge

First Fill-in Shell
Row 1 (RS): With RS of Rnd 1 facing, sc join dove in center st of any Shell, sc in next 15 sc, sc dec in last st of current Shell, marked sp of Rnd 2 Shell and first st of next Shell, sc in next 15 sc of next Shell, ending last sc in center st of Shell, turn. *(31 sc)*

Row 2: Ch 1, sc dec in first 2 sc, sc dec in next 2 sc, sc in next 10 sc, sc dec in next 3 sc, sc in next 10 sc, [sc dec in last 2 sc] twice, turn. *(25 sc)*

Row 3: Ch 1, sc dec in first 2 sc, sc dec in next 2 sc, sc in next 7 sc, sc dec in next 3 sc, sc in next 7 sc, [sc dec in next 2 sc] twice, turn. *(19 sc)*

Row 4: Ch 1, sc dec in first 2 sc, sc dec in next 2 sc, sc in next 4 sc, sc dec in next 3 sc, sc in next 4 sc, [sc dec in next 2 sc] twice, turn. *(11 sc)*

Row 5: Ch 1, sc dec in first 2 sc, sc dec in next 2 sc, sc in next sc, sc dec in next 3 sc, sc in next sc, [sc dec in next 2 sc] twice, turn. *(7 sc)*

Row 6: Ch 1, sc dec in first 2 sc, sc dec in next 3 sc, sc dec in next 2 sc, turn. Fasten off. *(3 sc)*

Next Fill-in Shell
Make 3.

Beg in same sc as last sc worked in previous Fill-in Shell, work same as First Fill-in Shell. At end of last Fill-in Shell, **do not** fasten off.

Headband
Rnd 1 (RS): Ch 1, evenly sp 14 sc across each Fill-in Shell around, change color to mustard, **join** *(see Pattern Notes)* in beg sc. *(56 sc)*

Rnd 2: Ch 1, sc in each sc around, join in beg sc.

Rnd 3: Rep rnd 2, changing color to dove.

Rnd 4: Rep rnd 2.

Rnd 5: Ch 1, **reverse sc** *(see Stitch Guide)* in each st around, join in beg sc. Fasten off.

Finishing
Pin edges of Shells tog, matching rows, and sew tog to form Crown. ●

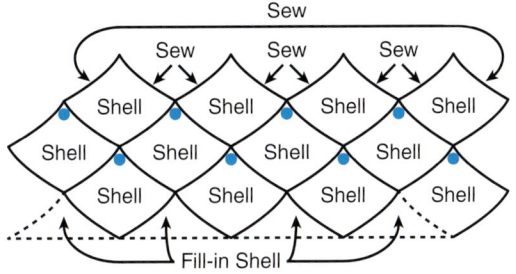

Slouchy Shell Patchwork Beanie
Assembly Diagram

KEY
● Marked Space

Mix It Up Scarf

Skill Level

 INTERMEDIATE

Finished Measurements

8 inches wide x 60 inches long, excluding Fringe

Materials

- Premier Yarns Anti-Pilling Everyday DK light (DK) weight acrylic yarn (3½ oz/273 yds/100g per ball):
  3 balls #1107-56 mustard
- Size G/6/4mm crochet hook or size needed to obtain gauge
- Tapestry needle
- Rustproof pins

Gauge

Square: 4 inches square

Pattern Notes

Before stitching begins, see Pattern Notes on page 3.

Scarf is made of Basic Squares and Textured Squares *(see instructions on pages 3 and 4)* worked with a join-as-you-go technique and with miters in opposite directions.

Weave in loose ends as work progresses.

Refer to Assembly Diagram for direction of Squares and joining beginning chains.

Squares 2 and 3 begin with 17 chains; Square 5 foundation row ends with 18 chains. When working next row of single crochet in chains, always work in **back bar of chains** *(see illustration on page 3).*

Join with slip stitch as indicated unless otherwise stated.

All Squares *(except Square 1)* are worked in ends of rows of Squares previously made.

"Corner point" is where 2 Squares meet.

Special Stitch

Single crochet join (sc join): Place a slip knot on hook, insert hook in indicated st, yo, pull up a lp, yo and draw through both lps on hook.

Scarf

Note: Work all joins with RS of previous Square facing.

Square 1

Work **Basic Square** *(see Pattern Notes).*

Square 2

Ch 17 *(see Pattern Notes),* referring to **Assembly Diagram** *(see Pattern Notes and Diagram)* and working in Square 1, work 16 sc across right edge *(beg ch-17 and 16 sc count as foundation row),* turn. Work rows 1–16 of **Textured Square** *(see Pattern Notes).*

Square 3

Ch 17, **join** *(see Pattern Notes)* in first row at top right corner of last Square made, ch 1, work 16 sc across *(beg ch-17 and 16 sc count as foundation row),* turn. Work rows 1–16 of Basic Square. At end of last row, **do not fasten off.**

Square 4

Ch 1, working down side of Square 3, work 16 sc across, sc in **corner point** *(see Pattern Notes),* work 16 sc across Square previously made *(33 sc count as foundation row),* turn. Work rows 1–16 of Textured Squares.

Square 5

Sc join *(see Special Stitch)* yarn in top right corner of Square 4, work 15 sc across top edge, ch 18 *(16 sc and*

18 chs count as foundation row), turn. Work rows 1–16 of Basic Square.

Square 6
Sc join yarn in top right corner of Square 3, work 15 sc across top edge, ch 1 in corner, work 16 sc up side of Square 5, turn. Work rows 1–16 of Textured Square.

Rep Squares 3–6 until 15 rows are worked.

Finishing

Edging
With RS of either short end facing, join yarn between 2 Squares, ch 1, work 16 sc across to next corner, [3 sc in next corner*, work 16 sc in each Square across to next corner] around, ending rep at *, work 16 sc across last Square, join in beg ch-1. Fasten off.

Fringe
Cut 108 10-inch strands *(54 for each end)*. Hold 3 strands tog, fold hank in half. From WS to RS, insert hook in any sc at short end, place folded end on hook and pull through, catching beg and end tails, pull ends through fold, pull ends to tighten knot.

Rep in each sc, working 18 Fringe across each short end.

Blocking
Lay Scarf on padded surface, sprinkle lightly with water, shape and pin to finished measurements with rustproof pins, allow to dry. ●

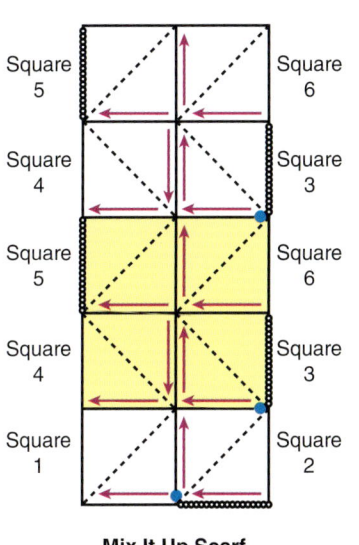

Mix It Up Scarf
Assembly Diagram

KEY
- - - Direction of miter
← Direction of sc
∘ Ch
● Placement of first sc

On Point Ski Hat

Skill Level

 ◼◼◼◻ INTERMEDIATE

Finished Measurements

20 inches in circumference x 10 inches tall

Materials

- Premier Yarns Anti-Pilling Everyday DK light (DK) weight acrylic yarn (3½ oz/273 yds/100g per ball):
  1 ball each #1107-14 teal and #1107-56 mustard
- Size G/6/4/mm crochet hook or size needed to obtain gauge
- Size K/10½/6.5mm hook
- Tapestry needle

Gauge

Square: 4 inches square; 5 inches across diagonal

Pattern Notes

Before stitching begins, see Pattern Notes on page 3.

Hat is made of 2 Tiers of 4 Basic Squares *(see instructions on page 3)* each with 2 Basic Squares for Ear Flaps. 2 Half-Squares fill in lower edge of Tier 1. Crown is formed by sewing Square sides together.

Work all Squares and Border with smaller hook; larger hook is for Braid and Tassel only.

Weave in loose ends as work progresses.

Refer to Assembly Diagram for position of Squares, joining beginning chains and sewing instructions.

Some Squares will begin with 18 chains. When working next row of single crochet in beginning chains, always work in **back bar of chains** *(see illustration on page 3).*

Join with slip stitch as indicated unless otherwise stated.

In Tier 2, do not fasten off color not in use; carry color not in use up sides, twisting new color with last color worked.

Special Stitch

Single crochet join (sc join): Place a slip knot on hook, insert hook in indicated st, yo, pull up a lp, yo and draw through both lps on hook.

Hat

Ear Flaps

With teal and **smaller hook** *(see Pattern Notes)*, work 2 **Basic Squares** *(see instructions on page 3).*

Tier 1

First Square

With mustard, **ch 18, holding first Ear Flap on point** (see Pattern Notes and Assembly Diagram) and working in ends of rows of right edge, **join** (see Pattern Notes) beg ch-18 in first row, ch 1, sc in same row and in each row across (beg ch-18 and 16 sc count as foundation row), turn. Work rows 1–16 of Square.

2nd Square

Join mustard in top of same Ear Flap, ch 1, working in ends of rows of left edge, sc in each row (16 sc), ch 18 (16 sc and ch-18 count as foundation row), turn. Work rows 1–16 of Square.

3rd Square

Join mustard in end of first row of Square just made, ch 18, holding 2nd Ear Flap on point and working in ends of rows of right edge, join beg ch-18 in first row, sc in each row (ch-18 and 16 sc count as foundation row), turn. Work rows 1–16 of Square.

4th Square

Rep 2nd Square.

Tier 2

*Note: Alternate teal and mustard, **changing colors** (see Stitch Guide and Pattern Notes) at end of each odd-numbered row of each Square.*

First Square

With RS of Tier 1 facing, join teal in top point of First Square, ch 1, working in ends of rows of left edge, sc in each row to last row, sc dec in last row, top point of Ear Flap and first row of next Square, sc in end of each rem row (31 sc), turn. Work rows 1–16 of Square.

2nd Square

Join teal in top point of next Square, working in ends of rows of left edge, sc in each row across, ch 1 (counts as a st), working in ends of rows of left edge of next Square, sc in end of each row, turn. Work rows 1–16 of Square.

3rd Square

Working in 3rd and 4th Squares of Tier 1, rep First Square.

4th Square

Join teal in top point of last Square of Tier 1, working in ends of rows of left edge, sc in each row across, ch 18, turn. Work rows 1–16 of Square.

Assembly

Referring to Assembly Diagram and photo, sew 4th Square of Tier 1 to First Square. Sew Squares of Tier 2 tog to form crown.

Half-Square
Make 2.

Row 1: With RS of bottom points of Ear Flaps up and working in ends of rows, join teal in first row at top of any Square in Tier 1, ch 1, sc in first 15 rows, sc dec in next row, join between Squares and first row of next Square, working in ends of rows of next Square, sc in each rem row.

Rows 2–8: Rep rows 2–8 of Square. At end of last row, fasten off.

Finishing

Border
Row 1: With RS facing and working in ends of rows around, **sc join** (see Special Stitch) teal in center of either Half-Square, sc in each row across to next Ear Flap (8 sc), [sc in first 15 rows of first edge of Ear Flap, 3 sc in last row (bottom point), sc in each rem row of other edge*, work 15 sc evenly across next Half-Square] twice, ending last rep at *, work 7 sc evenly across first Half-Square, join in beg ch-1. **Do not turn.**

Row 2: Ch 1, **reverse sc** (see Stitch Guide) in each st around, join in beg ch-1. Fasten off.

Continued on page 39

Sweet Dreams Baby Blanket

Skill Level

 **INTERMEDIATE**

Finished Measurements

39 inches wide x 40 inches long

Materials

- Lion Brand Baby Soft light (DK) weight acrylic/nylon yarn (5 oz/459 yds/140g per ball):
  - 3 balls #920-178 teal
  - 2 balls #920-100 white
- Size H/8/5mm crochet hook or size needed to obtain gauge
- Tapestry needle
- Stitch markers
- Rustproof pins

Gauge

Shell: 6½ inches wide

Pattern Notes

Before stitching begins, see Pattern Notes on page 3.

Blanket is made of Shells and Half-Shells worked with a join-as-you-go technique. Refer to Assembly Diagram for placement of Shells and marked stitches.

Weave in loose ends as work progresses.

Colors change at end of every odd-numbered row. Do not fasten off after each color change; carry yarn not in use up sides, twisting new color with last color worked.

Place markers where indicated and remove them as work progresses unless otherwise stated.

Special Stitch

Single crochet join (sc join): Place a slip knot on hook, insert hook in indicated st, yo, pull up a lp, yo and draw through both lps on hook.

Blanket

Row 1

Shell

Make 6.

Foundation row: With teal, ch 32.

Row 1 (WS): Working in **back bars of chs** (*see illustration on page 3*), sc in 2nd ch from hook and in each ch across, **change color** (*see Stitch Guide and Pattern Notes*) to white, turn. (*31 sc*)

Row 2: Ch 1, sc in first sc, [ch 1, sk next sc, sc in each of next 3 sc] 7 times, ch 1, sk next sc, sc in last sc. (*23 sc, 8 ch-1 sps*)

Row 3: Ch 1, sc in first sc, [ch 1, sk next ch-1 sp, sc in each of next 3 sc] 7 times, ch 1, sk next sc, sc in last sc, change color to teal, turn.

Row 4: Ch 1, sc in first sc, [hdc in ch-1 sp 2 rows below, sc in each of next 3 sc] 7 times, hdc in last ch-1 sp 2 rows below, sc in last sc, turn. (*23 sc, 8 hdc*)

Row 5 (first dec row): Ch 1, sc in first 2 sts, **sc dec** (*see Stitch Guide*) in next 2 sts [sc in next 2 sts, sc dec in next 2 sts] 6 times, sc in each of last 3 sc, change color to white, turn. (*24 sc*)

Row 6: Ch 1, sc in first sc, [ch 1, sk next sc, sc in each of next 2 sc] 7 times, ch 1, sk next sc, sc in last sc, turn. (*16 sc, 8 ch-1 sps*)

Row 7: Ch 1, sc in first sc, [ch 1, sk next ch-1 sp, sc in each of next 2 sc] 7 times, ch 1, sk last ch-1 sp, sc in last sc, change color to teal, turn.

Row 8: Ch 1, sc in first sc, [hdc in next ch-1 sp 2 rows below, sc in each of next 2 sc] 7 times, hdc in last ch-1 sp 2 rows below, sc in last sc, turn. *(16 sc, 8 hdc)*

Row 9 (2nd dec row): Ch 1, sc in first sc, sc dec in next 2 sts, [sc in next st, sc dec in next 2 sts] 6 times, sc in each of last 3 sts, change color to white, turn. *(17 sc)*

Row 10: Ch 1, sc in first sc, [ch 1, sk next sc, sc next sc] 8 times, turn. *(9 sc, 8 ch-1 sps)*

Row 11: Ch 1, sc in first sc, [ch 1, sk next ch-1 sp, sc in next sc] 8 times, change color to teal, turn.

Row 12: Ch 1, sc in first sc, [hdc in ch-1 sp 2 rows below, sc in next sc] 8 times, turn. *(9 sc, 8 hdc)*

Row 13 (3rd dec row): Ch 1, sc in first sc, [sc dec in next 2 sts] 8 times, change color to white, turn. *(9 sc)*

Row 14: Ch 1, sc in first sc, [ch 1, sk next sc, sc in next sc] 4 times, turn. *(5 sc, 4 ch-1 sps)*

Row 15: Ch 1, sc in each sc across, change color to teal, turn. Cut B. *(5 sc)*

Row 16: Ch 1, sc in first sc, sc dec in next 3 sc, sc in last sc, turn.

Row 17: Do not ch 1, sc in first sc, sk next sc, sc in last sc. Fasten off. **Place marker** *(see Pattern Notes)* in sp between sc for placement of first st of Shells. *(2 sc)*

Row 2

Note: *Refer to Assembly Diagram for correct placement of Shells and joining sts.*

Right Edge Half-Shell

Foundation row (RS): With RS of first Shell of previous row facing and working in ends of rows, **sc join** *(see Special Stitch)* teal in first row, sc in each row across, turn. *(15 sc)*

Row 1: Ch 1, sc in each sc across, change color to white, turn.

Row 2: Ch 1, sc in first sc, [ch 1, sk next sc, sc in each of next 3 sc] 3 times, ch 1, sk next sc, sc in last sc, turn. *(11 sc, 4 ch-1 sps)*

Row 3: Ch 1, sc in first sc, [ch 1, sk next ch-1 sp, sc in each of next 3 sc] 3 times, ch 1, sk last ch-1 sp, sc in last sc, change color to teal, turn.

Row 4: Ch 1, sc in first sc, [hdc in next ch-1 sp 2 rows below, sc in each of next 3 sc] 3 times, hdc in next ch-1 sp 2 rows below, sc in last sc, turn. *(11 sc, 4 hdc)*

Row 5 (first dec row): Ch 1, sc in first 2 sts, [sc dec in next 2 sc, sc in next 2 sts] 3 times, sc in last sc, change color to white, turn. *(12 sc)*

Row 6: Ch 1, sc in first sc, [ch 1, sk next sc, sc in each of next 2 sc] 3 times, ch 1, sk next sc, sc in last sc, turn. *(8 sc, 4 ch-1 sps)*

Row 7: Ch 1, sc in first sc, [ch 1, sk next ch-1 sp, sc in each of next 2 sc] 3 times, ch 1, sk last ch-1 sp, sc in last sc, change color to teal, turn.

Row 8: Ch 1, sc in first sc, [hdc in next ch-1 sp 2 rows below, sc in each of next 2 sc] 3 times, hdc in next ch-1 sp 2 rows below, sc in last sc, turn. *(8 sc, 4 hdc)*

Row 9 (2nd dec row): Ch 1, sc in first sc, [sc dec in next 2 sts, sc in next st] 3 times, sc in each of last 2 sc, change color to white, turn.

Row 10: Ch 1, sc in first sc, [ch 1, sk next sc, sc in next sc] 4 times, turn. *(5 sc, 4 ch-1 sps)*

Row 11: Ch 1, sc in first sc, [ch 1, sk next ch-1 sp, sc in next sc] 4 times, change color to teal, turn.

Row 12: Ch 1, sc in first sc, [hdc in next ch-1 sp 2 rows below, sc in next sc] 3 times, hdc in next ch-1 sp 2 rows below, sc in last sc, turn. *(5 sc, 4 hdc)*

Row 13 (3rd dec row): Ch 1, sc in first sc, [sc dec in next 2 sts] 4 times, change color to white, turn. *(5 sc)*

Row 14: Ch 1, sc in first sc, [ch 1, sk next sc, sc in next sc] 2 times, turn. *(3 sc, 2 ch-1 sp)*

Row 15: Ch 1, sc in each sc across, change color to teal, turn. Cut white. *(3 sc)*

Row 16: Ch 1, sc in each sc, turn.

Row 17: Do not ch 1, sc in first sc, sk next sc, sc in last sc. Fasten off. Place marker in sp between sc. *(2 sc)*

First Shell

Foundation row: Sc join teal in marked sp of Shell just worked, working in ends of rows across left edge, sc in first 14 rows, sc dec in last row of same Shell and first row of next Shell to join adjacent corners, working in ends of rows of next Shell, sc in each row across right edge, turn.

Work rows 1–17 of Shell.

Next Shell
Make 4.

Beg in last Shell worked and continuing in next Shell of previous row, rep first Shell just made.

Left Edge Half-Shell
Foundation row: Sc join teal in marked sp of last Shell worked, working in ends of rows across left edge, sc in next 14 rows, turn. *(15 sc)*

Rep rows 1–17 of Half-Shell.

Row 3

First Shell
Beg in marked sp of Right Edge Half-Square, work same as First Shell of Row 2.

Next Shell
Make 5.

Work same as Next Shell of Row 2.

Rows 4–18
[Rep Rows 2 and 3] 7 times, then rep Row 2. Do not remove markers of last 2 rows.

Row 19

First Fill-in Shell
Row 1 (RS): With RS facing, sc join teal in marked sp at top of Half-Shell, remove marker, working in ends of rows, sc in first 14 rows, sc in next marked sp, remove marker, working in ends of rows of next Shell, sc in next 14 rows, sc in next marked sp, do not remove marker, turn. *(31 sc)*

Row 2: Ch 1, sc dec in first 2 sc, sc in next 12 sc, sc dec in next 3 sc, sc in next 12 sc, sc dec in last 2 sc, turn. *(28 sc)*

Row 3: Ch 1, sc dec in first 2 sc, sc dec in next 2 sc, sc in next 8 sc, sc dec in next 3 sc, sc in next 8 sc, [sc dec in next 2 sc] twice, turn. *(21 sc)*

Row 4: Ch 1, sc dec in first 2 sc, sc dec in next 2 sc, sc in next 5 sc, sc dec in next 3 sc, sc in next 5 sc, [sc dec in next 2 sc] twice, turn. *(15 sc)*

Row 5: Ch 1, sc dec in first 2 sc, sc dec in next 2 sc, sc in next 2 sc, sc dec in next 3 sc, sc in next 2 sc, [sc dec in next 2 sc] twice, turn. *(9 sc)*

Row 6: Ch 1, sc dec in first 2 sc, sc dec in next 2 sc, sc in next sc, [sc dec in next 2 sc] twice, turn. *(5 sc)*

Row 7: Ch 1, sc dec in first 2 sc, sc in next sc, sc dec in last 2 sc, turn. *(3 sc)*

Row 8: Do not ch 1, sc dec in 3 sc. Fasten off. *(1 sc)*

Next Fill-in Shell
Make 5.

Row 1: Beg in last marked sp worked, rep Row 1 of First Fill-in Shell.

Rows 2–8: Work same as rows 2–8.

Edging
With RS of Row 1 facing, sc join teal in corner of first Shell *(see Assembly Diagram)*, sc evenly across side edge to top corner, 3 sc in corner, sc evenly sp across top edge to next corner, 3 sc in next corner, sc evenly across other side edge, working last sc in corner of Row 1, leave lower edge of Shells unworked. Fasten off. ●

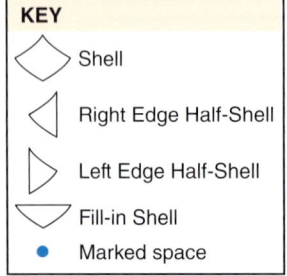

KEY

◇ Shell

◁ Right Edge Half-Shell

▷ Left Edge Half-Shell

▽ Fill-in Shell

● Marked space

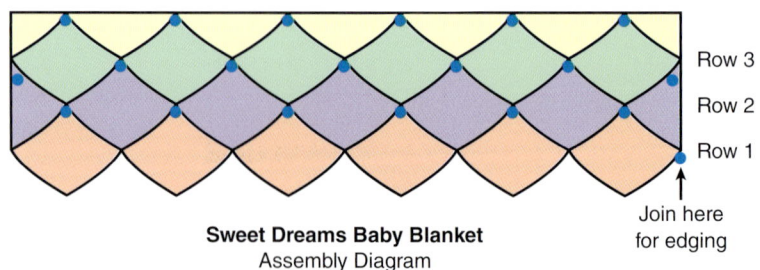

Row 3
Row 2
Row 1

Join here for edging

Sweet Dreams Baby Blanket
Assembly Diagram

Beanie Squared

Continued from page 22

Rnd 4: Ch 1, **reverse sc** *(see Stitch Guide)* in each sc around, join in beg ch-1. Fasten off.

Finishing

Pompom

Cut 18-inch strand of mocha, set aside. Wind mocha around cardboard 100 times. Carefully remove from cardboard, wind strand around center of bundle and tie tightly. Do not cut tail of tie.

Cut ends of lps, shake out, and trim evenly to desired length. Tie to top of Beanie with end tails. ●

On Point Ski Hat

Continued from page 34

Braid & Tassel
Make 2.

Cut 4 strands of teal, each 2½ yds long, draw all 4 strands through point of Ear Flap. With doubled strands held tog and larger hook, work as many chs as needed for 8 inches. Fasten off. Trim ends to 4 inches for Tassel. ●

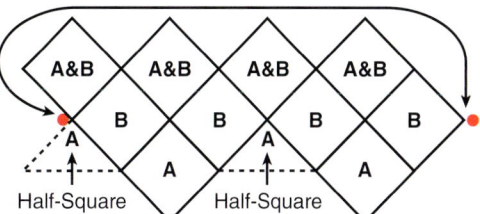

On Point Ski Hat
Assembly Diagram

KEY	
A Teal	
B Mustard	
● Joining points for seam	

ISBN: 978-1-64025-561-6

1 2 3 4 5 6 7 8 9

STITCH GUIDE

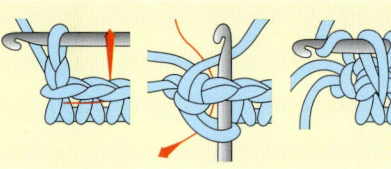

STITCH ABBREVIATIONS

beg	begin/begins/beginning
bpdc	back post double crochet
bpsc	back post single crochet
bptr	back post treble crochet
CC	contrasting color
ch(s)	chain(s)
ch-	refers to chain or space previously made (i.e., ch-1 space)
ch sp(s)	chain space(s)
cl(s)	cluster(s)
cm	centimeter(s)
dc	double crochet (singular/plural)
dc dec	double crochet 2 or more stitches together, as indicated
dec	decrease/decreases/decreasing
dtr	double treble crochet
ext	extended
fpdc	front post double crochet
fpsc	front post single crochet
fptr	front post treble crochet
g	gram(s)
hdc	half double crochet
hdc dec	half double crochet 2 or more stitches together, as indicated
inc	increase/increases/increasing
lp(s)	loop(s)
MC	main color
mm	millimeter(s)
oz	ounce(s)
pc	popcorn(s)
rem	remain/remains/remaining
rep(s)	repeat(s)
rnd(s)	round(s)
RS	right side
sc	single crochet (singular/plural)
sc dec	single crochet 2 or more stitches together, as indicated
sk	skip/skipped/skipping
sl st(s)	slip stitch(es)
sp(s)	space(s)/spaced
st(s)	stitch(es)
tog	together
tr	treble crochet
trtr	triple treble
WS	wrong side
yd(s)	yard(s)
yo	yarn over

YARN CONVERSION

OUNCES TO GRAMS		GRAMS TO OUNCES	
1	28.4	25	⅞
2	56.7	40	1⅔
3	85.0	50	1¾
4	113.4	100	3½

UNITED STATES		UNITED KINGDOM
sl st (slip stitch)	=	sc (single crochet)
sc (single crochet)	=	dc (double crochet)
hdc (half double crochet)	=	htr (half treble crochet)
dc (double crochet)	=	tr (treble crochet)
tr (treble crochet)	=	dtr (double treble crochet)
dtr (double treble crochet)	=	ttr (triple treble crochet)
skip	=	miss

Single crochet decrease (sc dec):
(Insert hook, yo, draw lp through) in each of the sts indicated, yo, draw through all lps on hook.

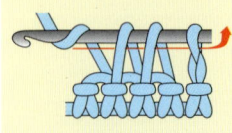

Example of 2-sc dec

Half double crochet decrease (hdc dec):
(Yo, insert hook, yo, draw lp through) in each of the sts indicated, yo, draw through all lps on hook.

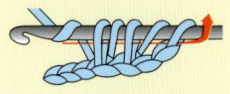

Example of 2-hdc dec

Reverse single crochet (reverse sc): Ch 1, sk first st, working from left to right, insert hook in next st from front to back, draw up lp on hook, yo and draw through both lps on hook.

Chain (ch): Yo, pull through lp on hook.

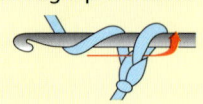

Single crochet (sc): Insert hook in st, yo, pull through st, yo, pull through both lps on hook.

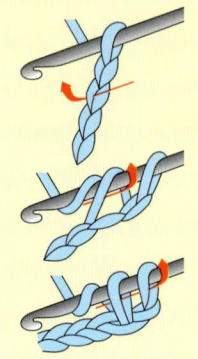

Double crochet (dc): Yo, insert hook in st, yo, pull through st, [yo, pull through 2 lps] twice.

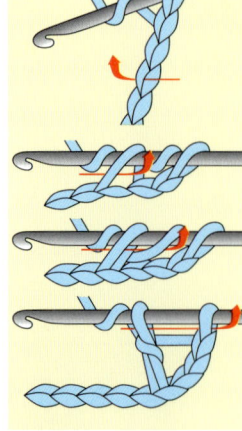

Double crochet decrease (dc dec): (Yo, insert hook, yo, draw lp through, yo, draw through 2 lps on hook) in each of the sts indicated, yo, draw through all lps on hook.

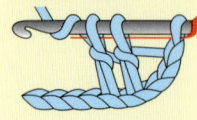

Example of 2-dc dec

Front loop (front lp) Back loop (back lp)

Front Loop   Back Loop

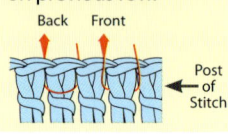

Front post stitch (fp): Back post stitch (bp): When working post st, insert hook from right to left around post of st on previous row.

Back   Front

Post of Stitch

Half double crochet (hdc): Yo, insert hook in st, yo, pull through st, yo, pull through all 3 lps on hook.

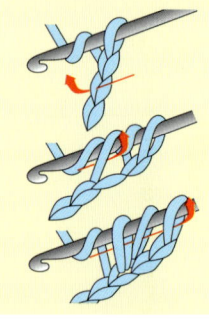

Double treble crochet (dtr): Yo 3 times, insert hook in st, yo, pull through st, [yo, pull through 2 lps] 4 times.

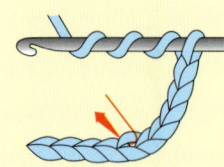

Treble crochet decrease (tr dec): Holding back last lp of each st, tr in each of the sts indicated, yo, pull through all lps on hook.

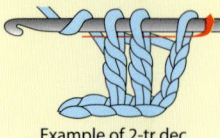

Example of 2-tr dec

Slip stitch (sl st): Insert hook in st, pull through both lps on hook.

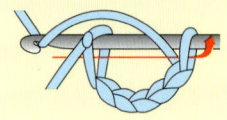

Chain color change (ch color change) Yo with new color, draw through last lp on hook.

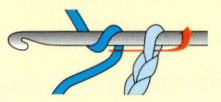

Double crochet color change (dc color change) Drop first color, yo with new color, draw through last 2 lps of st.

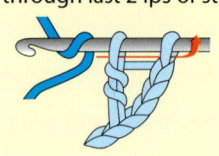

Treble crochet (tr): Yo twice, insert hook in st, yo, pull through st, [yo, pull through 2 lps] 3 times.

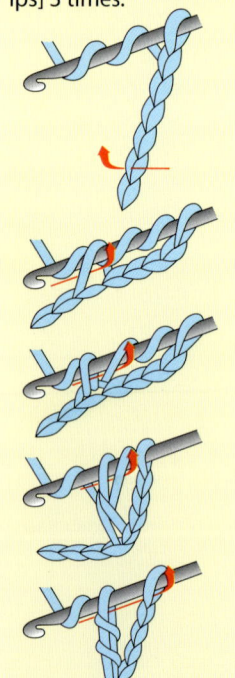